This Walker book belongs to:

- - - - - - - - - - - - - - - - - - - - - - - - - - - - - - - - - - -

- - - - - - - - - - - - - - - - - - - - - - - - - - - - - - - - - - -

*To each and every EXPERT – to those parents, grandparents, teachers, librarians, care-givers, child-development specialists, paediatricians, nurses, child psychologists and psychoanalysts who read over and looked over our work, talked to us, taught us and corrected us over and over again as we created this book for young children. We could not have created this book without you. THANK YOU! – R. H. H.*

*For Shelley, Yvonne, Nola and Margo*

*N. B. W.*

WALKER BOOKS
AND SUBSIDIARIES
LONDON • BOSTON • SYDNEY • AUCKLAND

First published 2012 by Walker Books Ltd
87 Vauxhall Walk, London SE11 5HJ

This eition published 2015

2 4 6 8 10 9 7 5 3 1

Text © 2012 Bee Productions, Inc.
Illustrations © 2012 Nadine Bernard Westcott

British Library Cataloguing in Publication Data:
a catalogue record for this book is available from the British Library

ISBN 978-1-4063-4540-7

www.walker.co.uk

# Who's In My Family?
## All About Our Families

Robie H. Harris

illustrated by Nadine Bernard Westcott

Families live in so many different kinds of places.
In cities. In towns. In the countryside.
In flats. In houses. Or on farms.
Families live near lakes. Near rivers. Near oceans.
In the desert. In the mountains. Or on grassy plains.

Families eat many different kinds of food for breakfast.
Some families eat bacon, eggs and bagels, and drink juice.

Some eat oranges and blueberry pancakes, and drink milk.

Some eat pitta bread, hummus, cucumber and olives.

Some families eat soup, shrimp dumplings and rice.

Some eat raspberries, bananas, muesli and yogurt.

Some eat papaya and burritos, and drink hot chocolate.

Families love being together. Families go to the market, to the library, to the doctor, to the dentist, to the park, to the zoo – and to so many other places together.

Families fly kites, ride bikes, play catch, get haircuts,
buy new shoes, visit friends or grandparents – and do
so many other things together.

People families are one kind of family. There are also animal families – squirrel families, polar bear families, sea lion families, zebra families, giraffe families, hippopotamus families, tiger families and so many other kinds of animal families.

Children are born into their families or adopted into their families. And most children live with and grow up in their families. Some families have one child. Some have two children.

Some families have three or four or more children. Some have twins. Some have triplets.

Many families have grown-ups and children in them.
Some families have only grown-ups.

Some families have a mummy and a daddy. Some have a mummy. Some have a daddy. Some have two mummies. Some have two daddies.

Some children live with their mummy part of the time and with their daddy part of the time.
Some children live with their daddy and a step-parent.
Some live with their mummy and a step-parent.

In some families, everybody's hair is the same – mostly wavy or mostly curly or mostly straight. In other families, people have different kinds and different colours of hair.

In some families, everybody has almost the same skin colour. In other families, people have different skin colours. In some families, people's eyes are different colours or different shapes. In other families, people have the same colour eyes or the same shape eyes.

Sometimes a grandparent or aunt or uncle lives with a child's family. And some children live in their grandparent's or aunt's or uncle's or foster parent's home.

Parents, sisters, brothers, grandparents, cousins, aunts and uncles can all be part of a child's family. Often, good friends or a pet can be part of a child's family too.

Families have happy times together.

Sometimes, children get a runny nose, a sore throat, a fever or a tummy-ache, or scrape a knee or cut a finger, or just feel bad.

Families help their children feel better and get well.

Parents and children help each other clean up, put away toys and feed their pets.

After supper, our puppy licks up EVERY crumb on the floor. Our puppy helps our family clean up!

Parents help their children have a bath, wash and dry their hair, brush their teeth, and get dressed for bed.

At night-time, our family also reads stories together. Sometimes we read the same story three times in a row!

Every day and every night and all around the world, families talk, laugh, sing, play, cuddle up, tell stories, read books, and make sure their children are healthy and safe and loved.

Most of all, and most of the time, and no matter what – children and grown-ups and their families really do love one another!

**Robie H. Harris** began her career as a teacher. Her interest in child-development issues and the experience of being a parent made her realize the importance of talking to children and teenagers about sometimes complicated and difficult topics. "I wanted my kids to stay healthy, so I had to give them accurate information," she says. Robie is the award-winning author of Let's Talk About Where Babies Come From; Let's Talk About Girls, Boys, Babies, Bodies, Families and Friends; Let's Talk About Sex; Who Has What?; What's in There?; and What's So Yummy? She lives in New York City, USA.

**Nadine Bernard Westcott** is the illustrator of more than a hundred books, including Who Has What?, What's in There? and What's So Yummy?. She now divides her time between illustrating books and designing her own unique line of textiles. Nadine lives in the USA in Nantucket, Massachusetts, with her husband, Bill.

## Look out for:

ISBN 978-1-4063-3677-1    ISBN 978-1-4063-4931-3    ISBN 978-1-4063-5803-2

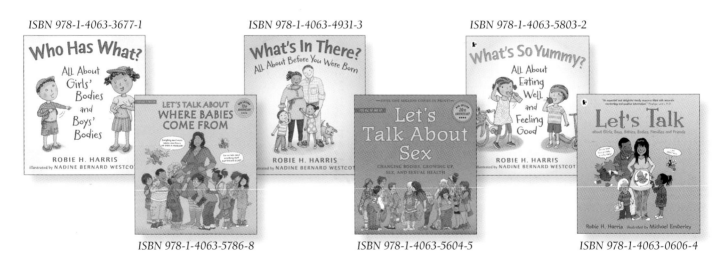

ISBN 978-1-4063-5786-8    ISBN 978-1-4063-5604-5    ISBN 978-1-4063-0606-4

*Available from all good booksellers*

*www.walker.co.uk*